Wheelch

Written by Dawn McMillan

CONTENTS

PEARSON

How Wheelchair Racing Started

Wheelchair racing is a fast and exciting sport. It combines an athlete's skill with wheelchair technology.

Wheelchair sport started in England after World War II. It was a great way for people injured in the war to exercise and have fun. However, it was thought that wheelchair racing might be bad for the competitors, so often there was a doctor or a nurse waiting at the finish line. In 1952, wheelchair athletes came from other countries to compete in wheelchair sports in England.

Cheri Becerra-Madsen of USA wins the women's 400-metre race at the 2000 Paralympic Games in Sydney.

A wheelchair basketball game in Rome, 1960

The first international games for people with disabilities was held alongside the Olympic Games in Rome, in 1960. In 1964, the games were held again, alongside the Tokyo Olympics, and this time, they were called the Paralympic Games. Today, the Paralympics immediately follow the Olympic Games and are held every four years.

Racing Chairs

When wheelchair racing started, the competitors used ordinary wheelchairs. The wheelchairs were heavy, and they had high backs. Today racing wheelchairs are very different. They are built for speed. They are long and low and light.

The main frame is made from lightweight aluminium tubing. The chairs have three wheels with two large angled wheels at the back. The wheels need to be light, so they are thin and made from carbon fibre. Wheels can have spokes, or they can be like a disk.

Pushrim

Spokes

A pushrim is attached to the outside of each back wheel. The pushrim is a ring made from lightweight metal tubing. It is covered with a small rubber tyre glued to the rim. The pushrim is used to make the chair move.

Camber

The angle of the wheels is called the camber. The camber keeps the chair stable and keeps the wheel away from the racer's arms.

Get Ready!

The wheelchair needs to be the perfect fit for the athlete. Most wheelchair athletes have their chair specially made for them. Track racers like shorter chairs so they have more room in the lanes. Road racers like longer chairs because it's easier to manage them on the bumpy roads.

The wheelchair racer athlete needs to be in the right seating position. Most athletes kneel in the racing chair. Some racing chairs have a sling instead of a seat. Wheelchair racers lean forward and keep their heads low. This improves the air flow under and around the chair, making it easier to go faster.

Track racers

Road racers

Design Features of the Racing Wheelchair

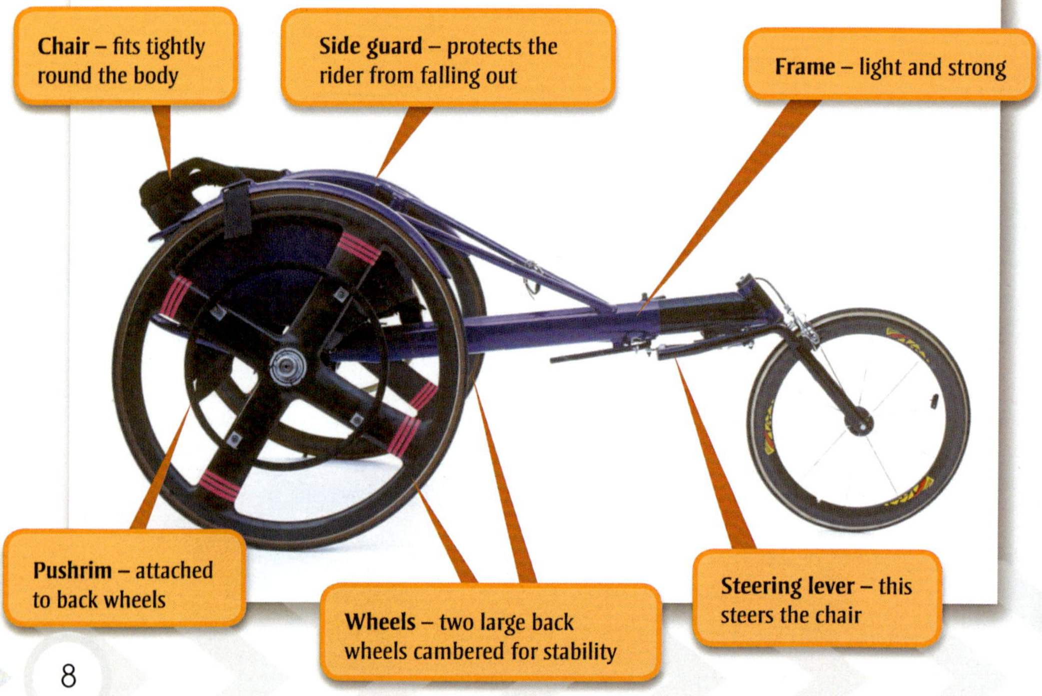

Chair – fits tightly round the body

Side guard – protects the rider from falling out

Frame – light and strong

Pushrim – attached to back wheels

Wheels – two large back wheels cambered for stability

Steering lever – this steers the chair

Many racers wear special gloves to protect their hands and give them grip. Some gloves have the three middle fingers in one big glove finger. The gloves have a hard surface under the thumb and on top of the middle fingers. The athletes put layers of tape around their gloves. The tape gives extra protection and better **grip. Some athletes like to make their own gloves.**

Push!

The racer moves the wheelchair by delivering force to the pushrim. The athlete's energy is transmitted to the chair. The pushrim acts like a gear. A smaller pushrim has poor acceleration but a high top speed. A larger pushrim has greater acceleration but a lower top speed. Pushing a racing chair is totally different from pushing an everyday wheelchair. For racing, the athlete hits the pushrims with a fist stroke. The thumb is used as a guide and the back of the hand pushes down.

Wheelchair racers in the Chicago Marathon, 2011

The wheelchairs are steered by a lever on the frame. The lever is like a rudder and points the front wheel in the direction that the racer wants to go. The racer changes direction by tapping the lever. A wireless computer on the wheelchair gives the racer information about speed and distance. The computer is solar powered.

How a Rider Pushes a Wheelchair

Races for Everyone

Wheelchair racers compete in:

- Sprints of 100m, 200m, 400m
- Middle distances of 800m and 1,500m
- Long distances of 5,000m and 10,000m
- Relay races, road races and the longest race of all – the 42km marathon

Wheelchair racers need to win because of their talent and not because they are less disabled than the other competitors. For important races, the athletes are divided into categories, depending on their disability. But in fun events, athletes from different categories often race each other.

There are also wheelchair racing competitions for children.

Some smaller athletes who have a high power-to-weight ratio are good short-distance sprinters. Larger, stronger athletes may do better in long-distance events. But long-distance racers need to be able to sprint too. They need to get into a good position at the start of the race, and they need to be able to go fast at the end.

Like all athletes participating in top-level sports, Paralympic wheelchair racers are tested for drug use. The testing ensures all competitors have an equal opportunity for success.

Rain did not stop competitors in the 1500m race at the 1996 Paralympic Games in Atlanta, USA.

Training and Fitness

Athletes work hard to keep their bodies in peak condition. They eat the right food, and they exercise to build strong muscles. Wheelchair racers need strong arms. Each athlete has different needs, so road and track training and gym programmes are designed to suit each person. Training rollers can be used to keep the athletes fit over winter. Pushing a chair on rollers is like pushing a chair on the road.

Wheelchair athlete James Lilly trains in his house in Chicago, USA, for the Sadler's Ultra Challenge, a 430-kilometre race across Alaska.

As well as being fit and strong, wheelchair racers learn about tactics. An important tactic is drafting.

Drafting is travelling closely behind another racer so that the racer in front blocks the air resistance. An athlete who is drafting uses less energy and can go faster. A racer may stay in the drafting position until he or she is ready to come out for the sprint to the finish.

Wheelchair racers drafting

Faster Still!

Wheelchair racers can travel up to 40 kilometres per hour on the track, but scientists and engineers are looking for ways to make racing wheelchairs go faster still. They are researching the best body positions for racing, and they are testing ways to make the chairs move faster through the air. Some engineers have made models with bullet-shaped shields to smooth the air flow around the racer. Now they are developing technology to gather data about power and force on the pushrim.

Wheelchair racing has come a long way from being a way for people with disabilities to exercise. Today it is a world-recognised sport. Maybe one day, it will become part of the Olympic Games. A wheelchair racer is a dedicated athlete, with a true love of the sport.

Index

Informational Explanation

Informational Explanations explain why something is the way it is or how something works.

How to Write an Informational Explanation

Step One

- Select a topic.
- Write down the things you know about the topic.
- Brainstorm the questions you need to ask.

Wheelchair Racing –Research Brief

How did wheelchair racing start?

How are racing chairs designed?

Why are road racing wheelchairs different from track racing wheelchairs?

How do athletes push their chairs?

How are races set up for competitions?

How do wheelchair racers train and get fit?

How will science and technology improve the sport?

Step Two

- Locate the information you need.
- Use different kinds of resources for your investigation:

Library   Internet   Television documentaries   Experts…

Take notes or make copies of what you find.

Step Three

Sort through your notes. Organise your information using headings.

Training and Fitness

Wheelchair athletes:
- eat the right foods
- exercise to build strong muscles
- do road or track training and gym programmes
- work on training rollers over the winter
- learn about tactics, such as drafting

Step Four

Use your notes to write your Explanation.

Include an **introduction** with an opening statement: *Wheelchair racing is a fast and exciting sport. It combines an athlete's skill with wheelchair technology.*

Include **visuals** such as…

Labels   Captions

Diagrams   Photographs

Your explanation could have...

a Contents page

CONTENTS

an Index

Index

Some informational explanations have a Glossary.

Guide Notes

Title: Wheelchair Racing

Stage: Advanced Fluency

Text Form: Informational Explanation

Approach: Guided Reading

Processes: Thinking Critically, Exploring Language, Processing Information

Written and Visual Focus: Captions, Labels, Index, Photographs, Diagrams

---

THINKING CRITICALLY
(sample questions)

Before Reading – Establishing Prior Knowledge
- What do you know about wheelchair racing?

Visualising the Text Content
- What might you expect to see in this book?
- What form of writing do you think will be used by the author?
- Look at the Contents page and Index. Encourage the students to think about the information and make predictions about the text content.

After Reading – Interpreting the Text
- What do you think is the purpose of this book?
- Do you think the introduction on page 2 effectively explains the idea behind the topic? Why or why not?
- What inferences can you make about how wheelchair athletes change the way some people see others with physical disabilities?
- Why do you think the pushrim is covered with rubber?
- How does the photograph on page 5 help the reader understand the purpose for angling the rear wheels? What inferences can you make about what would happen if the wheels were set in a 'straight up and down' position?
- What else do you think might help wheelchair racers go faster?
- What inferences can you make about how information from the computer may help the wheelchair racer?
- How would you create a visual to demonstrate the way athletes move their racing chairs as shown in the diagram on page 11?
- What inferences can you make about what type of categories might differentiate some competitors from others at the Paralympics?
- If you wanted to find out more about the division of wheelchair athletes into categories how would you go about it?
- Do you think training and fitness routines for all athletes are similar? Why or why not?
- What questions do you have after reading the text?
- Do you think the author effectively conveyed the information in this book? Why or why not? What helped you understand the information?